Frank Mills
MUSIC BOX DANCER COLLECTION
for Easy Piano

Easy piano arrangements by: Frank Mills, Ed McLean and Miles Jackson

Frank Mills has earned 20 gold and 10 platinum record awards.

He has appeared on countless television shows in Canada, USA, Japan and Europe and has hosted eight of his own specials for the CBC, CTV and ATV networks in Canada, including Christmas, Thanksgiving and concert performances.

For your **FREE** illustrated catalog containing all his recordings, piano books, videos and biography contact: MUSIC BOX DANCER Publications Ltd., 2600 John St, Unit 220, Markham, ON. Canada. L3R 3W3. Phone (905) 475-1848 / Fax (905) 474-9870

ISBN 0-921965-06-0

BALLET RUSSE

As featured on the recording: 25 Years of Piano Magic

Frank Mills
Arr: Edwin McLean

Dm
E♭
Dm
accel. poco a poco
E♭
Dm
E♭
decresc.
Dm
E♭
Dm
R.H.
L.H.
Tempo I
Gm
Dm
Gm
Dm
Gm
Dm
Gm7
A7
Dm
A
Dm
A7
Dm

CHICKADEE

As featured on the recording: Best of Frank Mills - Happy Music

Music by
FRANK MILLS

B♭
f
F
C7
F

to Coda
D.C. al Coda
CODA
C7
mf
F
Slowly
rit.
p
Ped.

A CLASICAL ROCK

As featured on the recording: Twentieth Anniversary

Music by
FRANK MILLS

Cm Fm G
f
Cm Fm G
Cm Fm
G
Cm
f
Cm/B♭
A♭7
G

Cm
Cm/B♭
A♭M7
G sus
G
ff
R.H.
R.H.
Cm
G
mf cresc.
Cm
G
Cm
G
Cm
ff

CONCERTO FOR PIANO

First Movement

As featured on the recording: Twentieth Anniversary

Music by
FRANK MILLS

B♭
F
B♭
F
C
mf
F
B♭
F
C
1.
F
2.
F

Dm
f
Csus4 C
Dm
Csus4 C
Fsus4 F
8
BbM7
ff
Csus4
C
F
f
Bb
F

Dm
f
G7
f
8
8
C7
8
8
mf
tr
cresc.
Ped.

8
f
mf
cresc. poco a poco
Play 3 Times
F
B♭
F
C
F
f
B♭
F
ff
B♭
F
8

CONCERTO FOR PIANO

Second Movement

As featured on the recording: Twentieth Anniversary

Music by
FRANK MILLS

Concerto 2nd Mov. 2/3 e.p.

Am7
Dm
Gm7
C7
to Coda
F
p
D.S. al Coda
CODA
F
p
Slowly
Gm7
poco rit.
C7
rit.
F
Ped.

CONCERTO FOR PIANO

Third Movement

As featured on the recording: Twentieth Anniversary

Music by
FRANK MILLS

Concerto 3rd Mov. 2/4 e.p.

Concerto 3rd Mov. 3/4 e.p.

Concerto 3rd Mov. 4/4 e.p.

FRANKS RAG

As featured on the recording: Best of Frank Mills- Happy Music

Music By:
FRANK MILLS

C7
F
C G/D C/E
B
F
C
C
F F/C Do C7
F
B♭

B♭ Bo F/C D7 G9 C7 F
B♭ Bo F/C D7 G7 C F
C
C D7
G7 C G

C
D7
F
F♯o
C/G
A7
D9
G7
C
F
F♯o
C
A7
1
D9
G7
C
2
D9
G7
C
F
F♯o
C
A7
D9
G7
C

FLAT BAROQUE

As featured on recording: 25 Years of Piano Magic

Music By:
FRANK MILLS

C
D A/C♯ D D E7 A
D A/C♯ D G D G Asus4 1 D 2 D
4 1 3 4 5
D
D Em A7 D Em A7
D G6 G Asus4 1 D
2 D G G Asus4 D
ritard..
Fine

HURON CAROL

As featured on the recording: A Traditional Christmas

Dynamically

Arr: Miles Jackson

B
Dm
Am Em7 Am
Dm
Am Em7 Am
Am Dm
Am
Em7 Am Em7
Am Em7
Am Dm
Am Em7
C
Am G/A
Am
Em7
Am
G/A Am
Em7 Am
Am G/A
Am
Em7
Am
Repeat and fade..

THE HAPPY SONG

As featured on the recording: Best of Frank Mills - Happy Music

Music By Frank Mills

F C G7 C
mf
8
G C F C
G7 C G C E7
f
Am D7 G

E7
D
G
C
F
C
G7
G
C
F
C
G7
C
1.G
C
loco
2.G
C
poco rit.

MARY'S SONG

As featured on the recording: Homeward

Music By:
FRANK MILLS

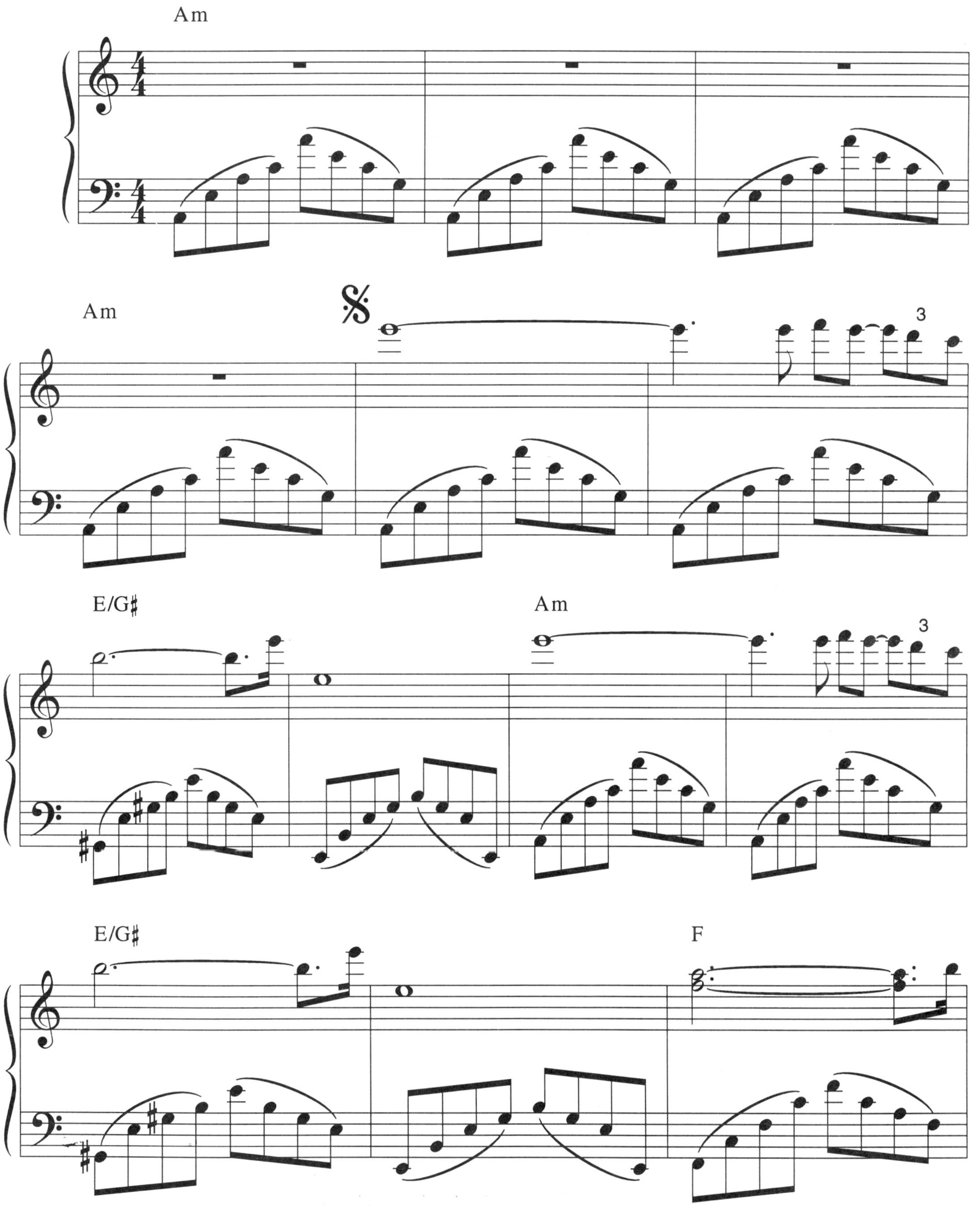

Selling agent: Music Box Dancer Publications Ltd., 2600 John St, # 220, Markham, ON. Canada. L3R 3W3

F
C
F
C
G7
C
al Coda
G7
C
F
C

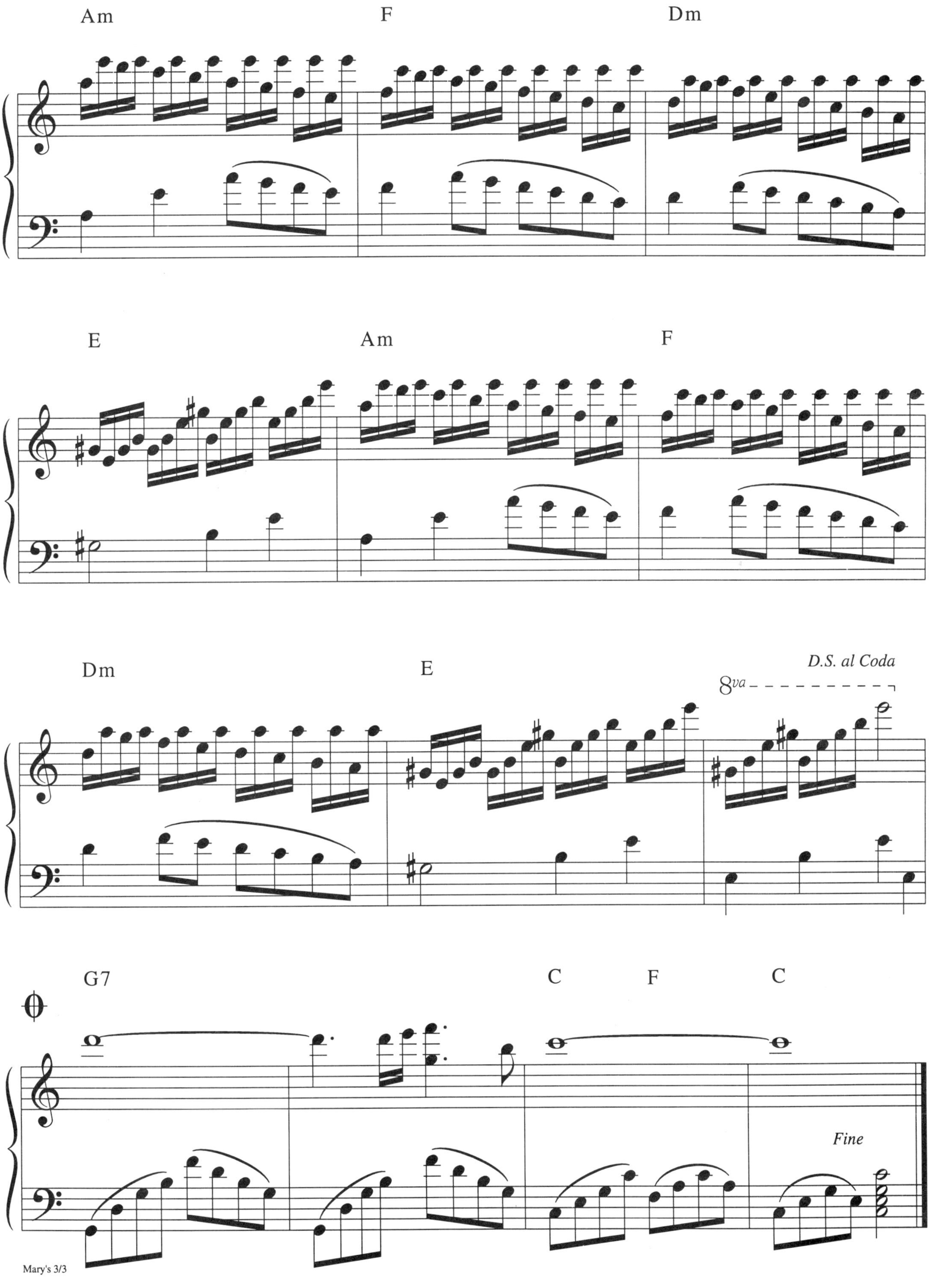
Am
F
Dm
E
Am
F
Dm
E
D.S. al Coda
8va
G7
C
F
C
Fine

LOVE ME, LOVE ME, LOVE

As featured on the recording: Best Of Frank Mills -Happy Music

Music & Lyrics by
Frank Mills
Arr: Edwin Mc Lean

Moderately Slow

A7
G
D
danced for joy when some-one put a
tell the world his sto-ry till
could-n't see the old man, I'm
pen-ny in. He sang:
death could ease the pain. He sang:
sure I heard him say: If you
D
A
G
D
LOVE ME, LOVE ME, LOVE;
Why did you ev-er leave me, girl? If you
D
A
G
D
LOVE ME, LOVE ME, LOVE;
Why did you ev-er go? If you
D
A
G
D
LOVE ME, LOVE ME, LOVE;
Why did you ev-er leave me, girl? If you
D
A
1.2.
G
D
D. C.
3.
G
D
LOVE ME, LOVE ME, LOVE;
Why did you ev-er go?
2. I
3. I
Why did you ev-er go?

THE LAND THAT I CALL HOME

As featured on the recording: Homeward

Music By:
FRANK MILLS

Thoughtfully..

Gm7 C B♭ F
F G7 Gm7 C F B♭maj7
F/A B♭ F Dm7 Gm7 C
F B♭maj7 F/A B♭ F C B♭ F
rit. Fine

MARY QUEEN OF SCOTS

As featured on the recording: Sunday Morning Suite

Frank Mills and M. Hoppe
Arr: Edwin McLean

Am
Dm
mf (f 2nd time)
E7
Am
F
C
Dm
1. E
2. E
D.C. al ⊕
rit. e dim.
⊕ Coda
E
Am
Em
Dm
F dim
Am
Ped.

MUSIC BOX DANCER

As featured on the recording: Best Of Frank Mills-Happy Music

Music By Frank Mills
This Arrangement by Bert Van der Hoek

Bright and lively

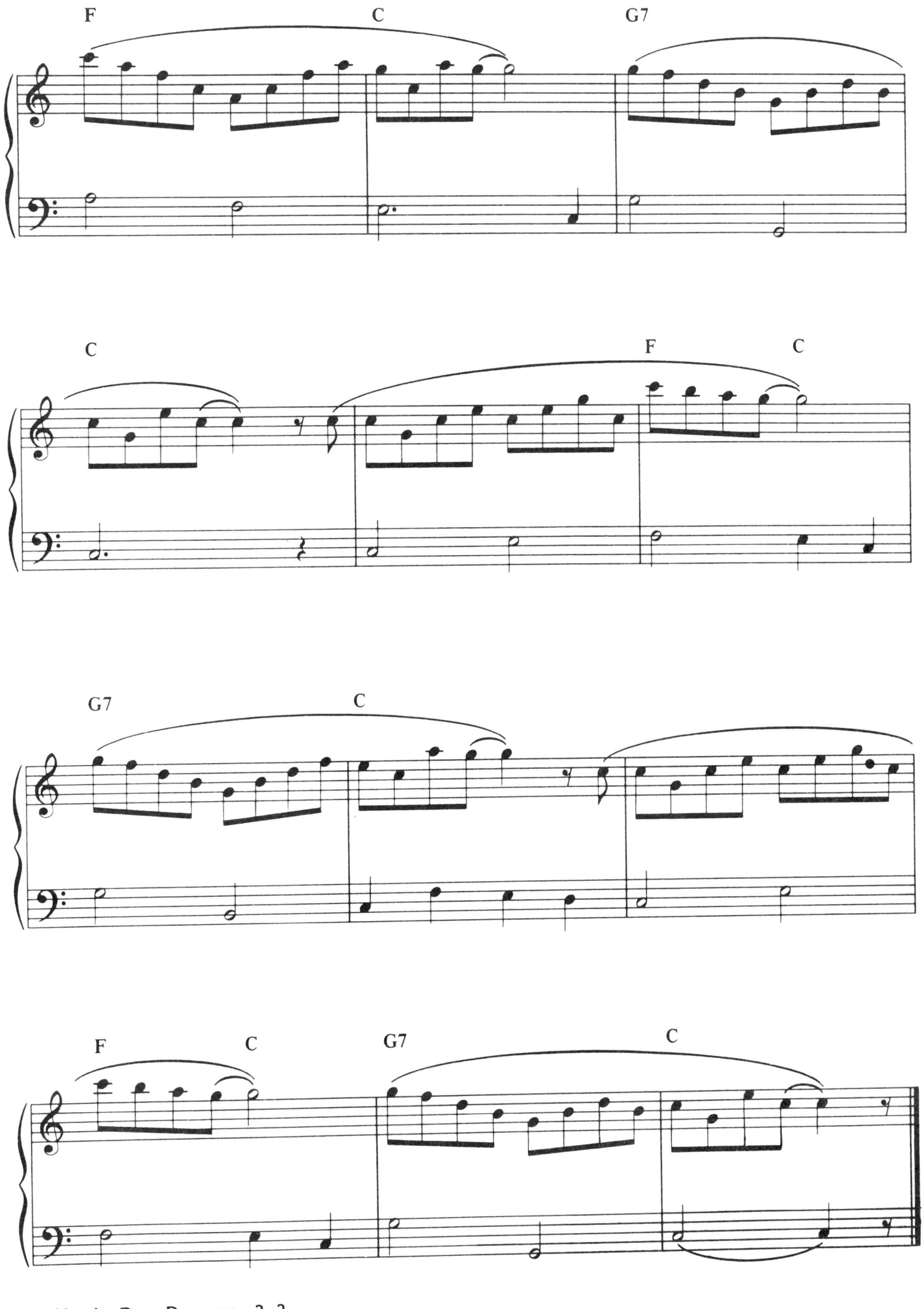
F
C
G7
C
F
C
G7
C
F
C
G7
C

PIANO LESSON NO. 5

as featured on the recording: Best of Frank Mills-Happy Music

Frank Mills
Arr: Edwin McLean

Var.2 "Swing"
F
mf (f 2nd time)
E7
F
D7-9
D7
G9
C7
F
1. G7
C7
2. G7
C

PLAISIR D'AMOUR

As featured on the recording: Prelude To Romance

G. P. Martini
Arr. Edwin McLean

F
G7
C
C#°
pp
cresc.
Dm
C#°
Dm
C
G7
f
C
F
C7
rit.
p
F
C7
F
C
G7
C7
F
Gm
F
C
rit.
p
8

PETER PIPER

As featured on the recording: 25 Years of Piano Magic

Music By Frank Mills

G
1.
C
2.
C
C
F
G
C
F
G
1.
C
2.
C
C
F
G
C
C
F
G
1.
C

2.
C
F
G
C
F
G
C
C
F
G
C
F
G
C

THE POET & I

As featured on the recording: Best Of Frank Mills - Happy Music

Lyrics by
Court Vines

Music by
Frank Mills

Arr: Edwin McLean

Slow with feeling

F
C7
F
world in beau- ti- ful rhyme.
love - li- est po- em I've heard.
hearts of the PO- ET AND I.
1.
To Coda
2.
Dm
— (2.The)
— But I find in the
Dm
A7
rhyme of the words in each line,
Dm
A7
Dm
Mem- 'ries of sea- sons with you;
Dm
F
C7
— Each haunt- ing phrase takes me

F
Dm
back to the days, to the thrill of the
Gm
A7
love we once knew.
Dm
Gm
C7
D. S. 𝄋 al Coda 𝄌
Verse} Tho'
CODA 𝄌
F7
B♭
Gm
F
C7
F

PRELUDE TO ROMANCE

as featured on the recording: Prelude to Romance

Music by
FRANK MILLS

Moderato

C
a tempo
mp
E7
Am
C/G
D7
C
to Coda
G9
C
D7
G7
ritard.
Fm
a tempo
mf
C

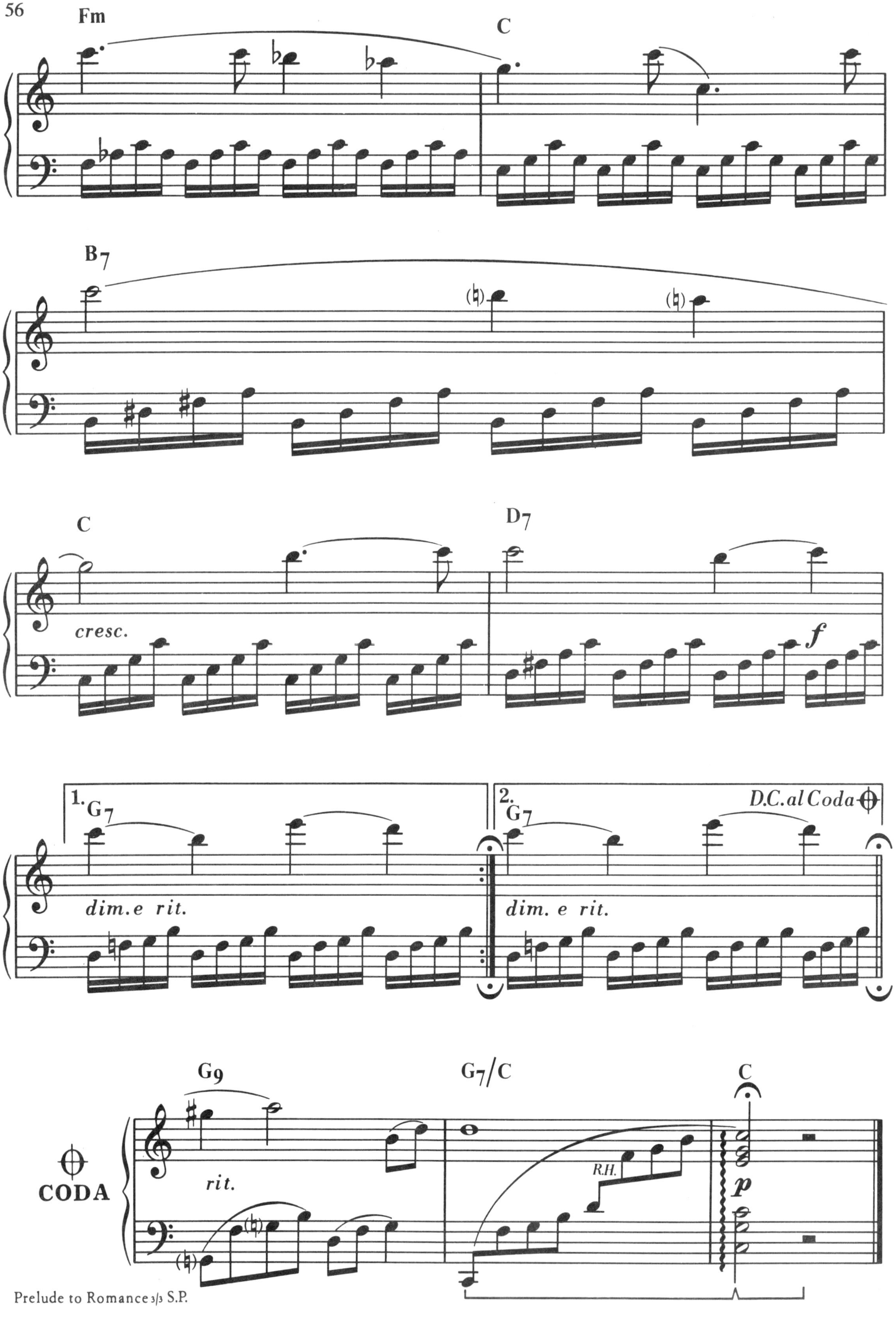
Fm
C
B7
C
cresc.
D7
f
1. G7
dim.e rit.
2. G7
dim. e rit.
D.C. al Coda
CODA
G9
rit.
G7/C
R.H.
C
p

REMINISCING WITH YOU

As featured on the recording: Homeward

Music By:
FRANK MILLS
& ANNIE REISLER

Old Time Waltz

G
G/D
C
G
C
C6
C
G
Dm7
G
F
C
C

C
G
Fmaj7
G
Em7
Am7
D7
G
C
D.S. al Coda
G
G/D
C
C
G
C
rit.
Fine

ROCKY MOUNTAIN SUNRISE

As featured on the recording: The Traveler

Music by
FRANK MILLS

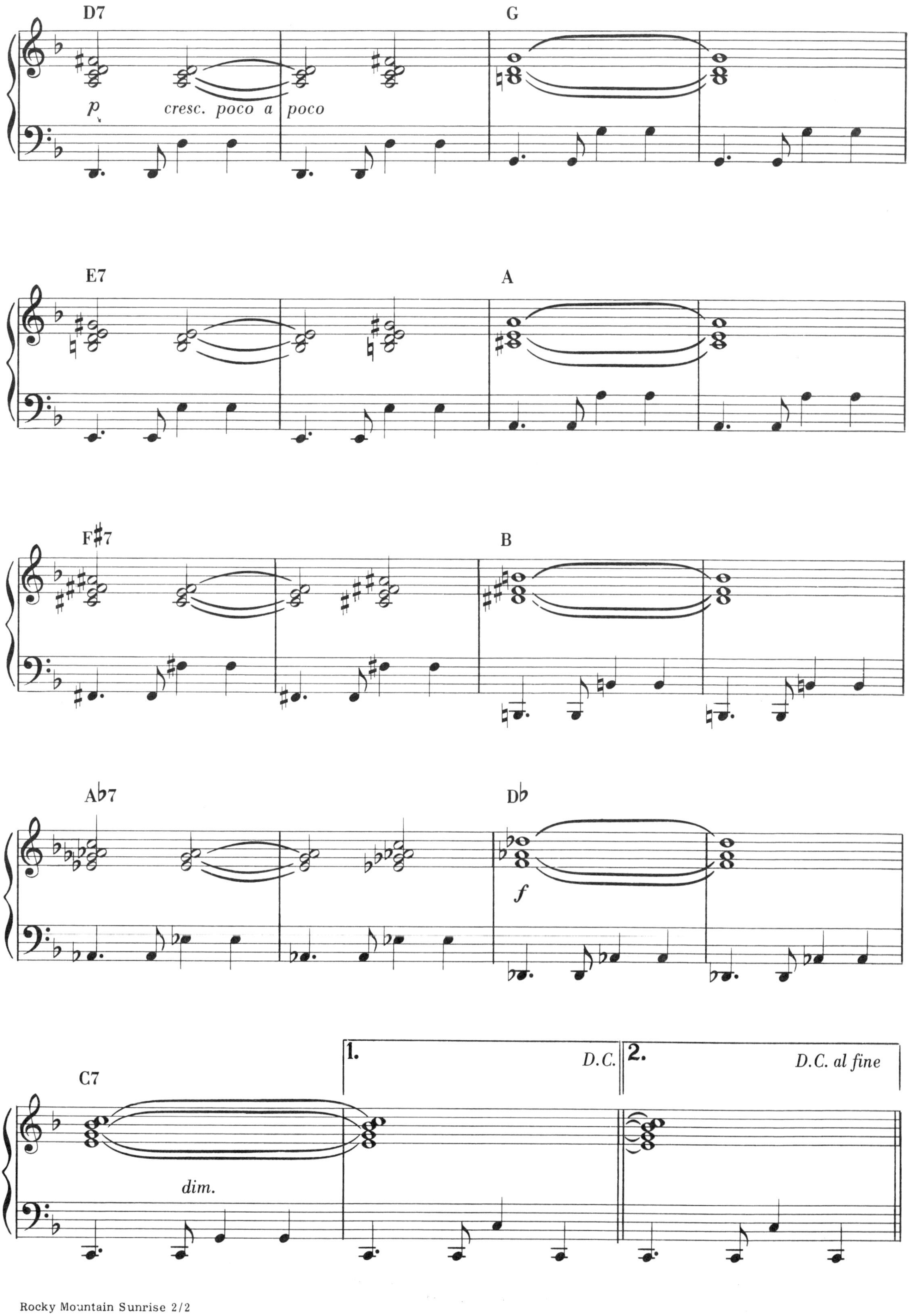
D7
G
p
cresc. poco a poco
E7
A
F♯7
B
A♭7
D♭
f
C7
dim.
1.
D.C.
2.
D.C. al fine

SEASCAPES

As featured on the albums: Transitions (variation 1), & Best of Happy Music (variation 2)

Music By:
FRANK MILLS
Arr: RALPH CRUICKSHANK

Moderato

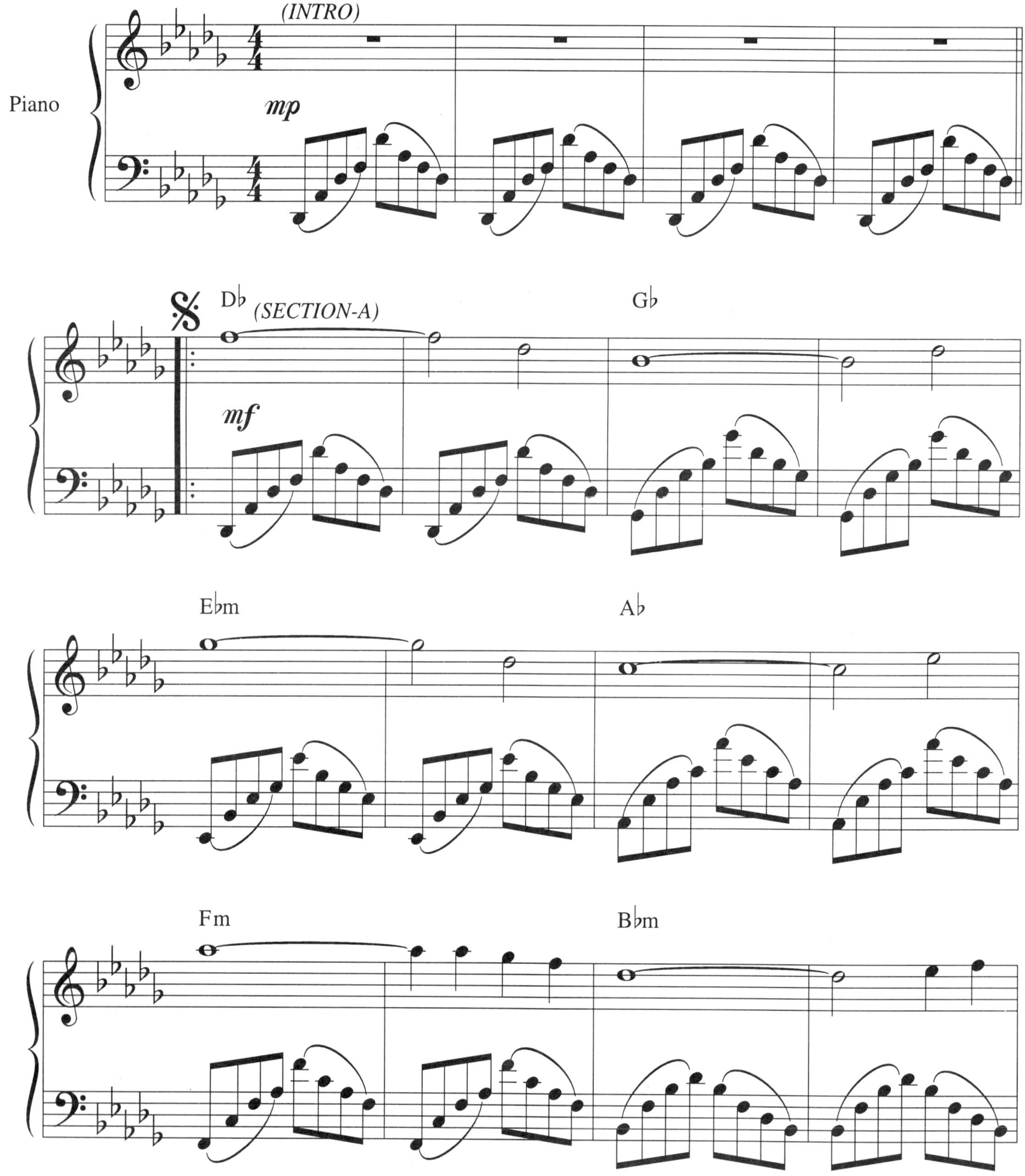

E♭m7
A♭
(SECTION-B)
G♭
D♭
f
G♭
D♭
Fm
B♭m
E♭m7
A♭
A♭7
D.S.-WITH REPEAT
2ND TIME FADE.
1
2
SECTION-A-1 TIME ONLY

SHADOWS OF THE DANCER

As featured on the recording: Transitions

Music by
FRANK MILLS
Arr: Edwin McLean

Allegro Moderato ♩ = 92

Cm
mf
a tempo
G
G7
Cm
G
G7
Fm
Cm
D7
1.3.4. etc.
G
Repeat ad lib. and fade
2.
G
D.S.
rit.

SUNDAY MORNING SUITE

As featured on the recording: Sunday Morning Suite

Frank Mills
Arr: Edwin McLean

1.
2.
mf
cresc.
f
1.
2.

WHEN YOU & I WERE YOUNG

As featured on the recording: Homeward

Arr. By: FRANK MILLS

C7 F B♭
3
F C7 F B♭
F C G7 C7
F B♭ F C7
1 F
2 F
Fine

THE ROAD TO HOME

As featured on the recording: Homeward

Music By:
FRANK MILLS

Moderato

D G D A
D Dsus4 D Dsus4
1
D F♯m G D
D F♯m D A/C♯ Bm A

D
F♯m
G
D
G
D
A
D
G
D
A
D
Dsus4
1, 2
3
D
Dsus4
D
Dsus4
D
Fine